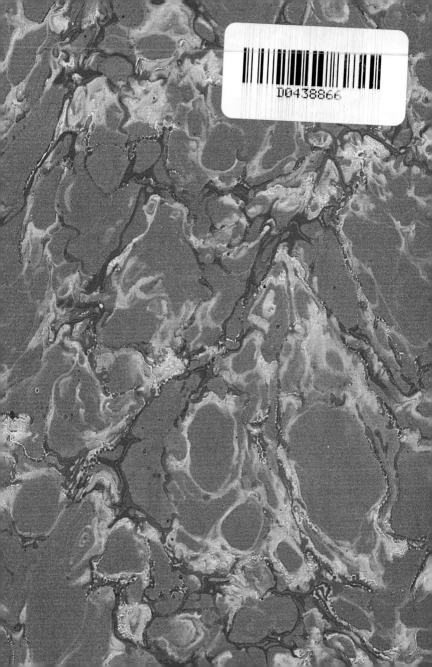

To: Faith - 1990-91

Love Always
    Sandy.

HEART
TH♥UGHTS

HEART THOUGHTS

A Treasury Of Inner Wisdom

Louise L. Hay

Compiled and Edited by
Linda Carwin Tomchin

Hay House, Inc.
Santa Monica, California

HEART THOUGHTS
A Treasury of Inner Wisdom
by Louise L. Hay

Copyright © 1990 by Louise L. Hay

The author of this book does not dispense medical advice nor prescribe the use of any technique as a form of treatment for physical or medical problems without the advice of a physician, either directly or indirectly. The intent of the author is only to offer information of a general nature to help you in your quest for physical fitness and good health. In the event you use any of the information in this book for yourself, which is your constitutional right, the author and the publisher assume no responsibility for your actions.

Library of Congress Catalog Card No. 90-55636
ISBN: 1-56170-000-2

Library of Congress Cataloging-in-Publication Data

Hay, Louise L.
    Heart thoughts: a treasury of inner wisdom / Louise L. Hay; compiled and edited by Linda Carwin Tomchin.
        p.   cm.
    ISBN 1-56170-000-2 $15.00
    1. Spiritual life. 2. Mental healing. I. Tomchin, Linda Carwin, 1947-
II. Title.
    BL624.H36   1990
    291.4′4—dc20   90-55636
                                                                     CIP

Page Composition and Design by Highpoint Type & Graphics, Claremont, CA

90 91 92 93 94 95 10 9 8 7 6 5 4 3 2 1

First Printing, October 1990

Published and Distributed in the United States by:

Hay House, Inc.
501 Santa Monica Boulevard
Post Office Box 2212
Santa Monica, California 90406 USA

Printed in the United States of America

Dedicated to Your Heart

Our hearts are the center of our power. I have learned that
we create easily and effortlessly when we let our thoughts
come from the loving space of the heart.
Claim your power now.

TABLE OF CONTENTS

INTRODUCTION

This book is a combination of meditations, spiritual treatments, and excerpts from my lectures. They focus on aspects of our day-to-day experiences and are meant to guide and assist us in particular areas with which we may be having difficulty.

When we feel like victims, we tend to isolate ourselves. We feel pain and fear, and we are always looking for someone else to save us, do it for us. We now have an opportunity to discover our abilities to respond to life, not as victims, but in ways that give us power. We will find that as we start to connect with what I call the *Inner Self*, we can contribute to improving the quality of our lives. It is a wonderful feeling to know that we don't have to be dependent on someone else, but that we have within us a tremendous capacity to make positive changes in our lives. It is a wonderfully liberating feeling.

Some people may be frightened by this new liberation, because it seems like *responsibility*. But responsibility merely means that we are able to respond to life. We are moving into a new age and a new order. It is time for us to release old beliefs and old habits. As we continue to learn and practice new beliefs and new methods of behavior, we will contribute harmoniously to the new order of the world.

Be patient with yourself. From the moment you decide to make a change until you have your demonstration, you may vacillate from the old to the new. Don't get angry with yourself. You want to build yourself up, not beat yourself up. You may want to refer to this book during those times when you are 'in-between' the old and the new. You may want to use the meditations and treatments on a daily basis until you build your confidence in your capability to make changes.

This is a time of awakening. Know that you are always safe. It may not seem so at first, but you will learn that life is always there for you. Know that it is possible to move from the old order into the new order safely and peacefully.

I love you,

Louise L. Hay

HEART THOUGHTS

*The more
we dwell on
what we
don't want,
the more we
get it.*

I am a yes person

I know I am one with all of Life. I am surrounded and permeated with Infinite Wisdom. Therefore I rely totally on the Universe to support me in every positive way. I was created by Life and given this planet to fulfill all my needs. Everything I could possibly need is already here waiting for me. This planet has more food on it than I could possibly eat. There is more money than I could ever spend. There are more people than I could ever meet. There is more love than I could possibly experience. There is more joy than I can even imagine. This world has everything I need and desire. It is all mine to use and to have. The One Infinite Mind, the One Infinite Intelligence always says "yes" to me. No matter what I choose to believe or think or say, the Universe always says "yes" to me. I do not waste my time on negative thinking or negative subjects. I choose my yes's with care. I choose to see myself and Life in the most positive ways. Therefore, I say yes to opportunity and prosperity. I say "yes" to all good. I am a "yes" person living in a "yes" world being responded to by a "yes" universe, and I rejoice that this is so. I am grateful and joyous to be one with Universal Wisdom and backed by Universal Power. Thank you God for all that is mine to enjoy in the here and now.

*Look in the
mirror and say:*

"I love
and accept myself
exactly as I am."

*What comes up
in your mind?
Notice how you feel.
This may be the
center of your
problem.*

I accept all the parts of myself

The biggest part of healing or making ourselves whole is to accept all of ourselves, all of the many parts of ourselves. The times when we did well, and the times when we didn't do so well. The times when we were terrified, and the times when we were loving. The times when we were very foolish and silly, and the times when we were very bright and clever. The times when we had egg on our faces, and the times when we were winners. All of these are parts of ourselves. Most of our problems come from rejecting parts of ourselves—not loving ourselves totally and unconditionally. Let's not look back on our lives with shame. Look at the past as the richness and fullness of Life. Without this richness and fullness we would not be here today. When we accept all of ourselves we become whole and healed.

*If you do not
love yourself
totally, wholly,
and fully,
somewhere
along the way
you learned not to.
You can unlearn it.
Start being kind
to yourself
now.*

I accept all that I have created for myself

I love and accept myself exactly as I am. I support myself, trust myself, and accept myself wherever I am. I can be within the love of my own heart. I place my hand over my heart and feel the love that is in my heart. I know there is plenty of room for me to accept myself right here and now. I accept my body, my weight, my height, my appearance, my sexuality, and my experiences. I accept all that I have created for myself. My past and my present. I am willing to allow my future to happen. I am a Divine, Magnificent Expression of Life, and I deserve the very best. I accept this for myself now. I accept miracles. I accept healing. I accept wholeness. And most of all, I accept myself. I am precious, and I cherish who I am. And so it is.

*We create
situations
and then we
give our power away
by blaming another
person for our
frustrations.
No person,
place or thing
has any power
over us.
We are the
only thinkers in
our minds.*

I express myself in positive ways

Usually if you are in an accident, and you are the one who is hit, you feel guilt on a deep level and perhaps have a need for punishment. There can be a lot of repressed hostility—feeling that you do not have a right to speak up for yourself. If you hit somebody, you are often dealing with unexpressed anger. This gives you an opportunity to express that anger. There is always more 'stuff' going on inside you. An accident is more than an accident. When an accident occurs, look within to see your own pattern and then bless the other person with love and release the whole experience.

*The moment
you say affirmations,
you are stepping out
of the victim role.
You are
no longer
helpless.
You are
acknowledging
your own
power.*

I am on the next step
to my healing

An affirmation is a beginning point. It opens the way. You are saying to your subconscious mind: *"I am taking responsibility."* *"I am aware there is something I can do to change."* If you continue to say the affirmation, either you will be ready to let whatever it is go, and the affirmation will become true; or it will open a new avenue to you. You may get a brilliant brainstorm; or a friend may call you and say: *"Have you ever tried this?"* You will be led to the next step that will help you with your healing.

*Affirmations
give your
subconscious mind
something to
work on
in the moment.*

I am open and receptive

When we do affirmations to create good in our lives, and there is a part of us that doesn't believe we are worth it, we are not going to manifest those affirmations. We will get to the point when we say: *"Affirmations don't work."* It has nothing to do with the affirmations, it is the fact that we don't believe we deserve.

*We must
become aware
of what it is
that we
believe.*

The answers within me come to my awareness with ease

If you are doing your affirmations in front of a mirror, always have a pad and pencil, so you can write down the negative messages that come to mind when you say them. You don't have to deal with the information right then. Later you can sit down, and, if you have a list of negative responses, you can begin to understand why you don't have what you say you want. If you are not aware of your negative messages, it is very difficult to change them.

*Anger is
a defense
mechanism.
You are
defensive
because you
are frightened.*

I release the past with ease and I trust the process of Life

Anger is a normal and natural process. Usually you get angry about the same things over and over again. When you are angry, you feel you don't have a right to express it, so you swallow it down. Swallowed anger tends to lodge in your favored part of the body and manifests itself through dis-ease. For years and years you keep packing your anger into that same place. So, in order to heal, let your true feelings out. If you cannot express them to the person directly involved, go to the mirror and talk to that person. Tell them everything: *"I'm pissed at you." "I'm frightened." "I'm upset." "You hurt me."* Just go on and on until all the anger is released. Then take a deep breath, look in the mirror, and ask: *"What is the pattern that created this?" "What can I do to make a change?"* If you can change the belief system inside that is creating this behavior, then you will not need to do it anymore.

*One of the
very worst things
we can do is to
get angry at
ourselves.
Anger only locks us
more rigidly into
our patterns.*

I am free to be me

Don't swallow your anger and have it settle in your body. When you get upset, give yourself a physical release. There are several methods to release these feelings in positive ways. You can scream in the car with the windows closed. You can beat your bed or kick pillows. You can make noise and say all the things you want to say. You can scream into a pillow. You can run, or play a game like tennis to help release the energy. Beat the bed or kick pillows at least once a week, whether you feel angry or not, just to release those physical tensions you store in your body.

*If we
wait until we
become perfect
before we love
ourselves we will
waste our lives.
We are
already perfect
right here and
right now.*

I am perfect exactly as I am

I am neither too much nor too little. I do not have to prove to anyone or anything who I am. I have come to know that I am the perfect expression of the Oneness of Life. In the Infinity of Life I have been many identities, each one a perfect expression for that particular lifetime. I am content to be who and what I am this time. I do not yearn to be like someone else for that is not the expression I chose this time. Next time I will be different. I am perfect as I am, right here and right now. I am sufficient. I am one with all of Life. There is no need to struggle to be better. All I need to do is to love myself more today than yesterday and to treat myself as someone who is deeply loved. As I am cherished by myself, I will blossom with a joy and beauty that I can barely begin to comprehend. Love is the nourishment that humans need to fulfill their greatness. As I learn to love myself more, I learn to love everyone more. Together we lovingly nourish an ever more beautiful world. We are all healed and the planet is healed too. With joy I recognize my perfection and the perfection of Life. And so it is.

*Life is
very simple.
Each one of us
creates our experiences
by our thinking
and feeling
patterns.
What we believe
about ourselves and
about life becomes
true for us.*

I create wonderful new beliefs for myself

These are some of the beliefs that I have created for myself over a period of time that really work for me:

I am always safe.

Everything I need to know is revealed to me.

Everything I need comes to me in the perfect
time, space and sequence.

Life is a joy and filled with love.

I prosper wherever I turn.

I am willing to change and to grow.

All is well in my world.

*Notice what
you are thinking
at this moment.
Do you want
this thought
to be creating
your future?
Is it
negative
or positive?
Just notice and
be aware.*

I experience the totality of possibilities within me

W hat does the totality of possibilities mean to you? Think of it as no limitations at all. Going beyond all limitations that we may set up. Let your mind go beyond what you thought was possible: *"It can't be done." "It won't work." "There's not enough." "This is in the way."* Or how often have you used these limitations? *"Because I'm a woman, I can't do this." "Because I'm a man, I can't do that." "I don't have the right education."* You hold onto limitations because they are important to you. But limitations stop you from expressing and experiencing the totality of possibilities. Every time you say, *"I can't,"* you are limiting yourself. Are you willing to go beyond what you believe today?

*If you
work where there
is love and joy
and laughter,
and you are
appreciated,
you are going to
do such a good job
and work twice as hard.
You will find that you
have more talents
and abilities than
you ever knew
you had.*

Our business is a Divine idea

Our business is a Divine idea in the One Mind, created out of Divine love and maintained and sustained by love. Every employee has been attracted by the action of love for it is his and her Divine right place here at this point in time and space. Divine harmony permeates us all and we flow together in a most productive and joyous way. It is the action of love that brought us to this particular place. Divine right action operates every aspect of our business. Divine Intelligence creates our products and services. Divine love brings to us those who can be helped by that which we so lovingly do. We release all old patterns of complaining or condemning for we know it is our consciousness that creates our circumstances in the business world. We know and declare that it is possible to successfully operate our business according to Divine principles, and we lovingly use our mental tools to live and experience our lives ever more abundantly. We refuse to be limited in any way by human-mind thinking. The Divine Mind is our business consultant and has plans for us which we have not yet dreamed. Our lives are filled with love and joy because our business is a Divine idea. And so it is.

*Rejoice
in other people's
successes because
there is plenty
for everyone.*

Our business is prosperous

We are one with the Universal Mind and therefore all wisdom and knowledge is available to us right here and right now. We are Divinely guided, and our business prospers, expands and grows. We now choose to release any negative thoughts about cash flow limitations. We open our consiousness to a quantam leap of prosperity by thinking and accepting that large amounts of money flood our bank account. We have plenty to use, to spare and to share. The law of prosperity keeps the flow of cash moving in abundant amounts. It pays our bills and brings us everything we need and more. Each of us within this organization prospers. We now chose to be living examples of prosperity consciousness. We live and work in comfort and ease and beauty. We have inner peace and security. We watch with joy and gratitude as we and this business continually grow and prosper far beyond our expectations. We bless this business with love. And so it is.

*There are
so many products
being sold on the basis
that you are not good enough
or acceptable enough unless
you use that product.
Messages of
limitation come from
many places. It does not
matter what other people say.
It is how we react and what
we choose to believe
about ourselves
that matters.*

This business is God's business

We are in partnership with the Divine Intelligence. We are not interested in the negative aspects of the outer business world for they have nothing to do with us. We expect positive results and we receive positive results. We attract to ourselves only those in the business world who operate on the highest level of integrity. Everything we do is done in the most positive way. We are continually successful in each and every project we do. All those with whom we do business in any manner are also blessed and prospered and are delighted to be connected with us. We are constantly grateful for the opportunites that are presented to us to help this planet and each person on it. We go within and connect with our higher intelligence and we are always led and guided in ways that are for the highest benefit of all concerned. All our equipment works perfectly. We are all healthy and happy. Everything is in harmony and flows in divine right order. All is well. We know this to be the truth for us. And so it is.

*In order to
change your life outside,
you must change
inside.
The moment
you are willing to change,
it is amazing how the
Universe begins
to help you.
It brings you
what you
need.*

All my changes are easy to make

When we begin to work on ourselves, sometimes things get worse before they get better. It is okay if that happens, it's the beginning of the process. It's untangling old threads. Just flow with it. It takes time and effort to learn what we need to learn. Don't demand instant change. Impatience is only resistance to learning. It means you want the goal without going through the process. Let yourself do it step by step. It will get easier as you go along.

Say:

"I am willing to change."

Are you hesitating?
Do you feel that
it is not true?
What is
the belief that
is in the way?
Remember
it is only a thought,
and a thought can
be changed.

When one door closes, another door opens

Life is a series of doors closing and opening. We walk from room to room having different experiences. Many of us would like to close some doors on old negative patterns, old blocks, things that are no longer nourishing or useful for ourselves. Many of us are in the process of opening new doors, and finding wonderful new experiences—sometimes a learning experience and sometimes a joyous experience. It is all part of life, and we need to know that we really are safe. It is only change. From the very first door that we open when we come to this planet to the very last door that we open when we leave this planet, we are always safe. It is only change. We are at peace with our own inner beings. We see ourselves as safe and secure and loved. And so it is.

*Gentle,
firm insistence,
and consistency
in what you
choose to think,
will make the changes
manifest quickly
and easily.*

I am willing to change

Clasp your hands together. Which thumb is on top? Now unclasp them and clasp them together again with the other thumb on top. How does that feel? Different? Maybe you have a reaction of *wrong*. Unclasp your hands again and clasp them the other way, and the second way, then the first. How does it feel now? Not quite so *wrong*? It is the same when you learn any new pattern. You need a little practice. You could do something the first time, and say: *"No, that's wrong"*, and never do it again, and you would go right back to being comfortable. If you are willing to practice a little bit, you will find that you can do the new thing. When you have something as important at stake as *you loving you*, it is well worth a little practice.

*When we
are ready to make
positive changes
in our lives,
we attract
whatever
we need
to help
us.*

I am willing to change and grow

I am willing to learn new things because I do not know it all. I am willing to drop old concepts when they no longer work for me. I am willing to see situations about myself and say: *"I don't want to do that anymore."* I know I can become more of who I am. Not a better person, because that implies that I am not good enough, but I can become more of who I am. Growing and changing is exciting, even if I have to look at some painful things inside me in order to do it.

*What is important in
this moment is
what you are
choosing to think and
believe and say right now.
These thoughts and words
will create your future.
Your thoughts form
the experiences
of tomorrow,
next week,
next month,
and
next year.*

It's only a thought, and a thought can be changed

How many times have you refused to think a positive thought about yourself? Well, you can refuse to think negative thoughts about yourself too. People say: *"I can't stop thinking a thought."* Yes, you can. You have to make up your mind that that is what you are going to do. You don't have to fight your thoughts when you want to change things. When that negative voice comes up, you can say: *"Thank you for sharing."* You are not giving your power over to the negative thought, and yet you are not denying that it is there. You are saying: *"Okay, you're there and thank you for sharing, and I'm choosing to do something else. I don't want to buy into that anymore, I want to create another way of thinking."* Don't fight your thoughts. Acknowledge them and go beyond them.

*Your parents were doing
the best they could
with the understanding
and awareness
that they had.
They could not teach
you anything that they
did not know.
If your parents did not
love themselves, there
was no way that they
could teach you
how to love
yourself.*

I create my future now

No matter what your early childhood was like, the best or the worst, you and only you are in charge of your life now. You can spend your time blaming your parents or your early environment, but all that accomplishes is keeping you stuck in victim patterns. It never gets you the good you say you want. Your current thinking shapes your future. It can create a life of negativity and pain or it can create a life of unlimited joy. Which one do you want?

*Children
always do
what we do.
You might examine
what is in the way
of your loving yourself
and be willing to
let it go.
You will be a
wonderful example
to your children.*

I communicate openly with my children

It is vitally important to keep the lines of communication open with children, especially in the teen years. Usually what happens when children start to talk about things, they are told over and over again: *"Don't say this." "Don't do that." "Don't feel that." "Don't be that way." "Don't express that." "Don't, don't don't!"* So children cut themselves off. They stop communicating. A few years later when they grow older, parents start to say: *"My children never call me."* Why don't they call? Because the lines of communication have been cut off at some point.

*Begin to listen
to what you say.
Don't say anything
that you don't
want to become
true for you.*

Everything I do is by choice

Remove the expression *"have to"* from your vocabulary and your thinking, because it is going to release a lot of self-imposed pressure on you. You can create tremendous pressure by saying: *"I have to get up." "I have to do this." "I have to, I have to."* Instead, begin by saying: *"I choose to. . ."* It puts a whole different perspective on your life. Everything you do is by choice. It may not seem so, but it is.

*Each
one of us
decides to incarnate
upon this planet at
particular points
in time and
space.
We have chosen
to come here to learn
a particular lesson that
will advance us on
our spiritual,
evolutionary
pathway.*

Let the spirit of love flow through you

Go back in time and remember the very best Christmas you ever had as a child. Bring the memory up in your mind and see it very clearly. Remember the sights, the smells, the tastes and touches, and the people who were there. What were some of the things that you did? If perchance you never had a wonderful Christmas as a child, make one up. Make it exactly as you would like it to be. As you think of this special Christmas, notice that your heart is opening. Perhaps one of the most wonderful things about that particular Christmas was the love that was present. Let the spirit of love flow through you now. Bring into your heart all the people you know and care about. Surround them with this love. Know that you can carry this special feeling of Christmas love and spirit with you everywhere and have it all the time, not only at Christmas. You are love. You are spirit. You are light. You are energy. And so it is.

*Loving
and approving
of yourself,
creating a space
of safety within you,
trusting, deserving and
accepting yourself
could create an
organized mind,
attract more
loving relationships,
bring about a new job,
and even allow your
body weight to
normalize.*

This day is a day of completion

Each moment of my life is perfect, whole and complete. With God nothing is ever unfinished. I am one with Infinite Power, Infinite Wisdom, Infinite Action, and Infinite Oneness. I awaken with a sense of fulfillment, knowing that I shall complete all that I undertake today. Each breath is full and comes to completion. Each scene I see is complete in itself. Each word I speak is full and complete. Each task I undertake, or each portion of that task, is completed to my satisfaction. I do not struggle alone in the wilderness of life. I release all belief in struggle and resistance. I know and affirm that I am one with the Infinite Power and therefore my way is made easy and smooth. I accept assistance from my many unseen friends who are always ready to lead me and guide me as I allow them to help. Everything in my life and in my work falls into place easily and effortlessly. Calls are completed on time. Letters are received and answered. Projects come to fruition. Others cooperate. Everything is on time and in perfect Divine right order. All is complete and I feel good. This day is a day of completion. I declare that it is so. My world is powerful and that which I declare and believe to be so is so. And so it is.

*Be aware
that you are
pure consciousness.
You are not lonely or
lost or abandoned.
You are one
with all
of Life.*

You are pure spirit

L ook within your very centered space and see the part of
you that is pure spirit. Pure light. Pure energy. Visualize all
your limitations falling away one by one, until you are safe, healed
and whole. Know that no matter what is going on in your life,
no matter how difficult things may be, at the very center of your
being you are safe, and you are whole. You always will be. Lifetime after lifetime, you are a shining spirit—a beautiful light.
Sometimes you come to this planet and cover your light and hide
it. But the light is always there. As you let those limitations go,
and as you recognize the true beauty of your being, you shine
brilliantly. You are love. You are energy. You are spirit. You are
the spirit of love shining brightly. Let your light shine.

*Every
time you
make a judgment
or a criticism, you are
sending something
out that is going
to come back
to you.*

I love being me

Can you imagine how wonderful it would be if you could live your life without ever being criticized by anyone? Wouldn't it be wonderful to feel totally at ease, totally comfortable? You would get up in the morning, and you would know you were going to have a wonderful day, because everybody would love you and nobody would criticize you or put you down. You would just feel great. You know what? You can give this to yourself. You can make the experience of living with you the most wonderful experience imaginable. You can wake up in the morning so thrilled to find yourself and feel the joy of spending another day with you.

*Critical people
often attract a lot of
criticism because it is
their pattern to criticize.
They often need
to be perfect at all times.
Do you know anyone
on this planet who
is perfect?*

I love and accept myself exactly as I am

We all have areas of our lives that we think are unacceptable and unloveable. If we are really angry with parts of ourselves, we often abuse ourselves. We use alcohol, drugs, cigarettes, we overeat, or whatever. We beat ourselves up. One of the worst ways we treat ourselves, which does more damage than anything else, is when we criticize ourselves. We need to stop all criticism. Once we get into the practice of doing that, it is amazing how we find we stop criticizing other people, because everyone is a reflection of us and what we see in another person we see in ourselves. When we complain about another person, we are really complaining about ourselves. When we can truly love and accept who we are, there is nothing to complain about. We cannot hurt ourselves and we cannot hurt another person. Let's make a vow that we will no longer criticize ourselves for anything.

*Some
of the things
we believe were
never true.
They were
someone else's fears.
Give yourself a chance to
examine your thoughts.
Change those that
are negative.
You are
worth it.*

I deserve good in my life

Sometimes when our inner messages are telling us that we are not allowed to be happy, or when we create good things in our lives and haven't changed those early messages, we will do something to thwart our happiness. When we don't believe that we deserve good, we will knock the pinnings out from under us. Sometimes we hurt ourselves, or have physical problems like falling, or have accidents. We have to start believing that we deserve all the good life has to offer.

*We learn
our belief systems as
very little children.
We then
move through life
creating experiences
to match our
beliefs.*

I deserve joy

Many of you believe that you deserve to live in an atmosphere of *"not good enough."* Start doing affirmations that you really deserve, and that you are willing to go beyond your parents' and your early childhood limitations. Look in the mirror and say to yourself: *"I deserve all good. I deserve to be prosperous. I deserve joy. I deserve love."* Open your arms wide and say: *"I am open and receptive. I am wonderful. I deserve all good. I accept."*

*Wherever
you go and
whomever you meet,
you will find your own
love waiting
for you.*

I follow the path of right action

In the Infinity of Life where I am, all is perfect, whole and complete. Knowing that I am one with the Source, and that I follow the path of right action, I am on principle at all times. I choose my thoughts to be in alignment with all that is for my highest good and greatest joy. My quality of life reflects this state that I presently want to be in. I love life. I love myself. I am safe at all times. All is well in my world.

*A rose is
always beautiful,
always perfect, and
ever changing.
This is
the way we are.
We are always perfect
wherever we are
in life.*

I am in the right place

Just as all the stars and planets are in their perfect orbit and in Divine right order, so am I. The heavens are in perfect alignment, and so am I. I may not understand everything that is going on with my limited human mind, however, I know that on the cosmic level, I must be in the right place, at the right time, doing the right thing. Positive thoughts are what I choose to think. This present experience is a stepping stone to new awareness and to greater glory.

Ask for help.
Tell Life what
you want,
and allow it
to happen.

Everything I need comes to me in the perfect time and space sequence

Doing affirmations, making wish lists, creating treasure maps, doing visualizations, writing in a journal can be compared to going to a restaurant. The waiter takes your order and then goes into the kitchen to give it to the chef. You sit there and do whatever you do because you assume that the food is on its way. You don't ask the waiter every two seconds: *"Is it ready yet? How are they making it? What are they doing in there?"* You place your order and know that your food will be served to you. It is much the same with what I call the *cosmic kitchen*. You place an order in the *cosmic kitchen* of the Universe and know it is being taken care of. It will come in the perfect time and space sequence.

*Release the
emotional attachment
to beliefs from the past
so that they don't
hurt you now.
If you live fully in the
moment, you cannot be
hurt by the past, no
matter what
it was.*

I am always safe

When you hold your emotions down, or hold things in, you create havoc within you. Love yourself enough to allow yourself to feel your emotions. Addictions, like alcohol, mask the emotions so that you *don't* feel. Allow your feelings to come to the surface. You may have to process quite a bit of old stuff. Start doing some affirmations for yourself so that you can do this easily, smoothly and comfortably. Affirm that you are willing to feel your true emotions and most importantly, keep telling yourself that you are safe.

*There
are people
looking for exactly
what you have to offer,
and
you are being
brought together on the
checkerboard
of life.*

I rejoice in my employment

My job is to express God. I rejoice in this employment. I give thanks for every opportunity to demonstrate the power of Divine Intelligence to work through me. Any time I am presented with a challenge I know it is an opportunity from God, my employer, and I quiet my intellect, turn within, and wait for words of treatment to fill my mind. I accept these blessed revelations with joy and know that I am worthy of my just reward for a job well done. In exchange for this exhilirating job, I am abundantly compensated. My fellow employees—all humankind—are supportive, loving, cheerful, enthusiastic, and powerful workers in the field of spiritual unfoldment whether they choose to be aware of it or not. I see them as perfect expressions of the One Mind diligently applying themselves to their jobs. Working for this unseen yet ever present Chief Operating Officer, the Ultimate Chairman of the Board, I know that my creative activity elicits financial abundance for the job of expressing God is ever rewarded. And so it is.

*Feel that
bounce in your step.
See your shining eyes.
The radiant you
is right here.
Claim it!*

I am healthy
and filled with energy

I know and affirm that my body is a friendly place to live. I have respect for my body and I treat it well. I connect with the energy of the Universe, and I allow it to flow through me. I have wonderful energy. I am radiant, vital and alive!

*Find an image
of something that
you really love:
flowers, a rainbow,
a special song, a sport
that you love. Let that
be the image that you
use every time you
start to scare
yourself.*

I am in harmony with nature

This I know and affirm for myself. I love and approve of myself. All is well in my world. I inhale the precious yet abundant breath of life and I allow my body, my mind, and my emotions to relax. There is no need for me to scare myself. I am in harmony with all of Life—the sun, the moon, the winds, the rain, the earth, and the movement of the earth. The power that resettles the earth is my friend. I am at peace with the elements. Nature's elements are my friends. I am flexible and flowing. I am always safe and secure. I know no harm can befall me. I sleep and wake and move in complete safety. Not only am I safe, my friends, family and loved ones are also safe. I trust in the power that created me to protect me at all times and under all circumstances. We create our own reality, and I create a reality for myself of oneness and security. Where I am there is always an island of safety. I am safe, it's only change. I love and approve of myself. I trust myself. All is well in my world.

*Today is
a very exciting
time of your life.
You are on a wonderful
adventure and will never go
through this particular
process again.*

I am on an endless journey through eternity

In the Infinity of Life all is perfect, whole and complete. The cycle of Life is also perfect, whole and complete. There is a time of beginning, a time of growth, a time of being, a time of withering or wearing out, and a time of leaving. These are all part of the perfection of Life. We sense it as normal and natural, and though saddened at times, we accept the cycle and its rhythms. Sometimes there is a sudden abrupt ending in mid-cycle. We are jarred and feel threatened. Someone died too young, or something was smashed and broken. Often thoughts that create pain remind us of our mortality—we, too, have an ending to our cycle. Shall we live out its fullness or will we too have an early ending? Life is ever changing. There is no beginning and no end, only a constant cycling and recycling of substance and experience. Life is never stuck or static or stale for each moment is ever new and fresh. Every ending is a new point of beginning.

*All the answers
to all the questions
you are ever going to
ask are right here
within you.
Every time you say,*

"I don't know,"

*you shut the door
to your own
wisdom.*

I breathe in love and flow with life

A re you expanding or contracting? When you expand your thinking, your beliefs, and everything about yourself, the love flows freely. When you contract, you put up walls and shut yourself off. If you are frightened or threatened or feeling something is not right, begin to breathe. Breathing opens you up. It straightens your spine. It opens your chest. It gives your heart room to expand. By practicing breathing you drop the barriers and begin to open up. It is a beginning point. Instead of going into total panic, take a few breaths, and ask yourself: *"Do I want to contract or do I want to expand?"*

*This is
a new day.
Begin anew to
claim and create
all that is
good.*

I express my true being

I see myself having a consiousness of oneness with the presence and power of God. I see myself ever aware of the power of God within me as the source of everything I desire. I see myself confidently calling upon the Presence to supply my every need. I love all expressions of God unconditionally, knowing the truth of all that is. I walk through life with the happy companionship of my Godself and joyfully express the goodness I am. My wisdom and understanding of spirit increases and I express more fully each day the inner beauty and strength of my true being. Divine order is ever present in my experience and there is plenty of time for all that I choose to do. I express wisdom, understanding, and love in all my dealings with others and my words are Divinely guided. I see my consciousness of spiritual abundance expressing as plenty—plenty to use for good in my world. I see myself expressing the creative energy of Spirit in my work; writing and speaking words of truth easily and with a depth of understanding and wisdom. Fun, uplifting ideas flow through my consciousness for joyful expression, and I follow through on the ideas received, bringing them into full manifestation. And so it is.

*It is
your birthright
to express yourself
in ways that are
fulfilling to
you.*

I freely express who I am

I am indeed blessed. There are wonderful opportunities to be myself, to express myself as who I really am. I am the beauty and joy of the Universe expressing and receiving. I surround myself with Divine honesty and justice. I know that Divine right action is taking place and whatever the outcome is, it is perfect for me and everyone concerned. I am one with the very power that created me. I am wonderful. I rejoice in the truth of my being. I accept it as so and let it be. I say, so be it, and know that all is well in my wonderful, wonderful world right here and right now. And so it is.

*If you
want love and
acceptance from your
family, then you must
have love and
acceptance
for them.*

I bless my family with love

Not everyone has the special family that I have, nor do they have the extra opportunites to open their hearts in the way my family does. We are not limited by what the neighbors think nor by society's prejudices. We are far more than that. We are a family that comes from love, and we accept with pride every unique member. I am special and I am worthy of love. I love and accept each member of my wonderful family, and they, in turn, love and adore me. I am safe. All is well in my world.

*How are
you treating
elderly people now?
What you give out is
what you are going
to find when you
get older.*

I have loving compassion for my father

If you have any 'stuff' with your father, do a meditation in your mind, and talk with him, so that you can clean up old issues. Forgive him or forgive yourself. Tell him that you love him. Get cleaned up in your mind, so that you can move into feeling more deserving for yourself.

*Sometimes
when our lives
are magnificent, we have
anxiety that something
bad is going to
happen to take
it all away.
I call it running anxiety.
Anxiety is fear and not
trusting yourself.
Just recognize it as the
part that is used to us being
upset about something
and thank it for
sharing and
let it go.*

I am always perfectly protected

Remember, when a fearful thought comes up, it is trying to protect you. Isn't that what fear is all about? When you become frightened, your adrenalin pumps up to protect you from danger. Say to the fear: *"I appreciate that you want to help me."* Then do an affirmation about that particular fear. Acknowledge and thank the fear but don't give it importance.

*We do not have to
know how to
forgive.
All we have to do
is be willing
to forgive.
The
Universe will
take care of the how.*

I forgive all past experiences

When the word *forgiving* is mentioned, who comes to your mind? Who is the person or what is the experience that you feel you will never forget, never forgive? What is it that holds you to the past? When you refuse to forgive, you hold onto the past, and it is impossible for you to be in present time. It is only when you are in the present that you can create your future. Forgiving is a gift to yourself. It frees you from the past, the past experience, and past relationships. It allows you to live in present time. When you forgive yourself and forgive others, you are indeed free. There is a tremendous sense of freedom that comes with forgiveness. Often you need to forgive yourself for putting up with painful experiences and not loving yourself enough to move away from those experiences. So love yourself, forgive yourself, forgive others and be in the moment. See the old bitterness and the old pain just roll off your shoulders as you let go, and the doors of your heart open wide. When you come from a space of love you are always safe. Forgive everyone. Forgive yourself. Forgive all past experiences. You are free.

*The more self-hatred
and guilt we have,
the less our
lives work.
The less self-hatred
and guilt we have,
the better our
lives work—
on all levels.*

I am free

I am pure spirit and light and energy. I see myself as being free. I am free in my mind. I am free in my emotions. I am free in my relationships. I am free in my body. I feel free in my life. I allow myself to connect to that part of me that is pure spirit and is totally free. I release all of my limitations and my human-mind fears. I no longer feel stuck. As I connect with that spirit within me, that part of me that is pure spirit, I realize that I am far more than my personality, or my problems, or my dis-ease. The more I connect with this part of me, the more I can be free in every area of my life. I can choose to be that part of my spirit that is totally free. If I can be free in one area, I can be free in many areas. I am willing to be free. The part of me that is pure spirit knows how to lead me and guide me in ways that are very beneficial to me. I trust the spirit part of me and know that it is safe to be free. I am free in my love for myself. I let that love for myself flow as freely as possible. It is safe to be free. I am spirit, and I am free. And so it is.

Happiness
is feeling
good about
yourself.

I can do what I want

I am grown up now! I can do anything that I want to do. Whenever I do what I want to do, something wonderful happens to me. Saying "no" to someone else can be nurturing to myself. As I nurture myself I find more fun in my world. I am allowed to have fun. The more fun I have, the more other people love me. I love and approve of myself. I feel good about myself. All is well in my fun-filled world.

*We are
on an endless
journey through eternity.
We have lifetime
after lifetime.
What we
don't work out
in one life, we will
work out in
another.*

There is no death

Our spirit can never be taken from us for it is the part of us that is eternal. No argument can take it from us. No dis-ease can take it from us. No loss of relationship can take it from us. No death can take it from us for spirit is eternal. It is the part of us that goes on forever. All the people we know who have left the planet are still here in pure essence and pure spirit. They always have been, they are now, and they always will be. It is true that we will not connect with their physical bodies again, but when we leave our bodies, our spirits will connect. There is no loss. There is no death. There is only a cycling and recycling of energies—a changing of form. When we connect with our spirits, we go beyond all petty things. Our understanding is so great. Our spirit, our soul, the very essence of who we are is always safe, always secure, and always alive. And so it is.

*A tragedy
can turn out to
be our greatest good
if we will approach
it in ways from
which we can
grow.*

I let the light of my love shine

When we are in pain, or afraid, or grieving, and we see a light in the darkness, we don't feel so alone. Let's think of this light as someone's love shining. It gives us warmth and comfort. Each of us has the light of our love within us. We can let our light shine, so it will comfort us and be a great comfort to others. We all know people who have passed on. See now their light shining, and let their light and love surround us and comfort us. Each one of us has an infinite supply of love to give. The more we give, the more there is to give. Yes, sometimes it hurts to feel, but thank God we can feel. Let the love come radiating from our hearts. Be comforted and be at peace. And so it is.

Feel
your heart
opening and know
that there is room
in there for
you.

I treat myself with unconditional love

If your childhood was full of fear and battling, and you mentally beat yourself now, you are continuing to treat your inner child much the same. The child has no place to go within you. Love yourself enough now to go beyond your parents' limitations. They did not know any other way to train you. You have been a good little child for a long time, doing exactly what mommy and daddy taught you. It is time for you to grow up and make adult decisions that support and nourish you.

*Guilt
never makes
anyone feel better, nor
does it change a situation.
Stop feeling guilty.
Let yourself out
of prison.*

I forgive myself for any wrong doing

So many of you live under a heavy cloud of guilt. You always feel wrong. You are not doing it right. You are apologizing all the time. You will not forgive yourself for something you did in the past. You manipulate others as you once were manipulated. Guilt does not solve anything. If you really did something in the past that you are sorry about, stop doing it! If you can make amends to the other party, do it. If not, then don't do it again. Guilt looks for punishment and punishment creates pain. Forgive yourself and forgive others. Step out of your self-imposed prisons.

*Everything
in your life,
every experience,
every relationship
is a mirror
of the
mental pattern
that is going on
inside you.*

I am a harmonious being

I am a center in the Divine Mind, perfect, whole and complete. All my affairs are Divinely guided into right action with perfect results. Everthing I do, say or think is in harmony with truth. There is perfect and continuous right action in my life and in my affairs. It is safe for me to change. I release all thoughts or vibrations of confusion, chaos, dis-harmony, dis-respect, or dis-trust. These thoughts are eliminated from my consciousness completely. I am harmoniously linked with everyone with whom I am in contact. People love working and being with me. I express my thoughts, feelings and ideas, and they are easily welcomed and comprehended by others. I am a loving, joyful person, and everybody loves me. I am safe. I am welcomed with joy wherever I am. All is well in my world, and life gets better all the time.

*Search
your heart
for injustices
that you still harbor,
forgive them and
let them go.*

I am centered in truth and peace

No matter where I am there is only spirit, God, Infinite good, Infinite wisdom, Infinite harmony and love. It cannot be otherwise. There is no duality. Therefore, right here and right now in my workplace I declare and affirm that there is only Infinite harmony, wisdom and love. There are no problems that do not have solutions. There are no questions without answers. I now choose to go beyond the problem to seek the Divine right action solution to any discord that may seem to appear in the true harmonious atmosphere of this business. We are willing to learn and grow from this seeming discord and confusion. We release all blame and turn within to seek the truth. We are also willing to release whatever pattern that may be in our consciousness which has contributed to this situation. We choose to know the truth and the truth sets us free. Divine wisdom, Divine harmony and Divine love reign supreme within me and around me and within and around each and every person in this office. This business is God's business and God is now directing, leading and guiding our movements. I declare for myself and for each and every person in this business peace, security, harmony, and a deep sense of love for the self and the joyous willingness to love others. We are centered in truth and live in joy.

*Healing
means to make
whole, to accept all parts
of ourselves, not just
the parts we like,
but all
of us.*

I can heal myself on all levels

This is a time of compassion and a time of healing. Go within and connect with that part of yourself that knows how to heal. It is possible. Know that you are in the process of healing. This time you discover your healing abilities—abilities that are strong and powerful. You are incredibly capable. So be willing to go to a new level to find abilities and capabilities that you were not aware of, and not to cure a dis-ease, but to truly heal yourself on all possible levels. You are spirit, and being spirit, you are free to save yourself. . .and the world. And so it is.

Dis-ease
breeds in unforgiveness.
Forgiveness has nothing to
do with condoning behavior.
The very person you
find it hardest
to forgive
is often the one
you need to let go of
the most. I have found that
forgiving and releasing
resentment will help
to dissolve even
cancer.

I am a magnet for miracles

Unknown and unexpected good is coming my way this day. I am far more than rules and regulations—restriction and limitations. I change my consciousness and miracles occur. Within every medical establishment there is a growing number of practitioners who are enlightened and on a spiritual pathway. I now attract these people to me wherever I am. My mental atmosphere of love and acceptance is a magnet for small miracles every moment of the day. Where I am, there is a healing atmosphere, and it blesses and brings peace to all. And so it is.

*If we don't
make internal changes,
the dis-ease either comes
back or we create
another dis-ease.*

I let my whole being vibrate with light

Look deep within the center of your heart and find that tiny pinpoint of brilliantly colored light. It is such a beautiful color. It is the very center of your love and healing energy. Watch as your pinpoint of light begins to pulsate and grow until it fills your heart. Let it move through your body from the top of your head to the tips of your toes, and through the tips of your fingers. You are absolutely glowing with this beautiful colored light, which is your love and your healing energy. Let your body vibrate with this light. You can even say to yourself: *"With every breath I take, I'm getting healthier and healthier."* Feel the light cleansing your body of dis-ease. Let the light radiate from you into your room, into the world and into your special place in the world. See everything whole. You are important. You do count. What you do with the love in your heart does matter. You do make a difference. And so it is.

*Every
illness holds
a lesson for
us to
learn.*

My hands are powerful
healing tools

The laying on of hands is normal and natural. It is a very ancient process. You know that if your body hurts, the first thing you do is place your hand over the spot to make it feel better. So allow yourself to give energy to yourself. Take a deep breath and release tension, or fear, or anger, or pain, and let the love flow from your heart. Let your heart open so you can receive the love that is coming into your body. Your body knows exactly what to do with this healing energy and how to use it. See the light of love coming from your heart—a beautiful, beautiful light. Let that love come rolling from your heart, through your arms, and into your hands. That light penetrates your very being with compassion, understanding and caring. See yourself as whole and healed. Your hands are powerful. You deserve love. You deserve to be at peace. You deserve to feel safe. You deserve to be cared for. Allow yourself to receive. And so it is.

*We need
to do more than
just treat the symptom.
We need to eliminate the
cause of the dis-ease.
We need to go within
ourselves where
the process of
illness began.*

Every hand that touches me is a healing hand

I am a precious being and loved by the Universe. As I increase the love I have for myself, so too does the Universe mirror this, increasing love ever more abundantly. I know that the Universal Power is everywhere, in every person, place and thing. This loving, healing power flows through the medical profession and is in every hand that touches my body. I attract only highly evolved individuals on my healing pathway. My presence helps to bring out the spiritual, healing qualities in each practitioner. Doctors and nurses are amazed at their abilities to work as a healing team with me.

*The body,
like everything
else in life, is a mirror
of your inner thoughts
and beliefs.
Every cell
responds to every
single thought you think
and every word
you speak.*

I listen to my body's messages

In this world of change I choose to be flexible in all areas. I am willing to change myself and my beliefs to improve the quality of my life and my world. My body loves me in spite of how I may treat it. My body communicates with me, and I now listen to its messages. I am willing to get the message. I pay attention and make the necessary corrections. I give my body what it needs on every level to bring it back to optimum health. I call upon an inner strength that is mine whenever I need it. And so it is.

*Good health
is having no fatigue,
having a good appetite,
going to sleep and
awakening easily,
having a good
memory,
having good
humor, having
precision in thought
and action, and being
honest, humble,
grateful and
loving.
How healthy
are you?*

My body, mind and spirit are a healthy team

The body is always talking to you. What do you do when you get a message from the body such as a little ache or pain? Usually, you run to the medicine cabinet or the drugstore and take a pill. In effect you say to the body: *"Shut up! I don't want to hear you. Don't talk to me!"* That is not loving the body. When you get the first ache or pain, or the slightest thing seems to go wrong, sit down, close your eyes, and very quietly ask yourself: *"What is it I need to know?"* Listen a few minutes for the answer. It may be as simple as, *"Get some sleep."* Or it may be stronger. If you want your body to work well for you for a long time, then you need to be a part of the body, mind and spirit healing team.

*Some people
don't know how
to say "no."
The only way
they know how
to say "no,"
is to be ill.*

I accept what is best for me

If I threw a hot potato at you, what would you do with it? Would you catch it? Would you hold it while it was burning your hand? Why would you even catch it? Why don't you just step out of the way? It is possible to refuse anything, even a gift. Are you aware of that?

*If you
want to move
from where you are,
thank your present home
for being there for you.
Appreciate it.
Don't say:
"Oh, I hate this place,"
because then you are not
going to find something
you really love.
Love where
you are, so you
can open yourself
to a wonderful
new place.*

My home is a peaceful haven

Look at your home. Is it a place that you really love to live in? Is it comfortable and joyous, or is it cramped and dirty and always messy? If you don't feel good about it, you are never going to enjoy it. Your home is a reflection of you. What state is it in? Go and clean out your closets and refrigerator. Take all the stuff in the closets that you haven't worn in a period of time, and sell it, give it away or burn it. Get rid of it so that you can make room for the new. As you let it go, say: *"I'm cleaning out the closets of my mind."* Do the same with your refrigerator. Clean out all the foods and scraps that have been there for awhile. People who have very cluttered closets and cluttered refrigerators have cluttered minds. Make your home a wonderful place to live in.

*Money is
energy; it is an
exchange of services.
It is matter and form. It has
no meaning of itself except
what we give it and
believe about it.
We have
so much 'stuff'
about money, but it
really is about what
we believe we
deserve.*

My income is constantly increasing

The quickest way to increase your income is to do the mental work. What can you do to help yourself? You can either choose to attract or repel money and other forms of prosperity. Complaining never works. You have a cosmic mental bank account, and you can deposit positive affirmations and believe you deserve, or not. Affirm: *"My income is constantly increasing. I am worth prospering."*

*You can spend
your time griping
and begrudging the
things that went wrong
or how you are not good
enough or you can
spend your time
thinking about
joyous experiences.
Loving yourself and
thinking joyful, happy
thoughts is the quickest
route you can take to
create a wonderful life.*

I have unlimited potential

In the Infinity of Life where we all are, all is perfect, whole and complete. We rejoice in knowing we are one with the Power that created us. This Power loves all its creations including us. We are the beloved children of the Universe and have been given everything. We are the highest form of life on this planet and have been equipped with all that we need for every experience we shall have. Our minds are always connected to the One Infinite Mind, therefore, all knowledge and wisdom are available to us as we believe it is so. We trust ourselves to create for ourselves only that which is for our highest good, greatest joy and perfect for our spiritual growth and evolution. We love who we are. We are particularily delighted with the incarnation we have chosen this lifetime. We know that we can from moment to moment shape and reshape our personalities and even our bodies to further express our greatest potential. We rejoice in our unlimitedness and know that before us lie the totality of possibilities in every area. We trust totally in the One Power and we know all is well in our world. So be it!

*Be gentle, kind
and comforting with
your inner child as you
uncover and release the old,
negative messages
within you. Say:*

"All my changes are
comfortable, easy
and fun."

I love myself totally in the now

L ove is the biggest eraser there is. Love erases even the deepest imprinting because love goes deeper than anything. If your childhood imprinting was very strong, and you keep saying: *"It's all their fault. I can't change,"* you stay stuck. Do a lot of mirror work. Love yourself in the mirror from the top of your head to the tips of your toes. Dressed and naked. Look into your eyes and love you and your child within.

*Each one of us
is always working
with the three-year
old child within us.
Most of us, unfortunately,
spend our time
yelling at that child,
and then wondering
why our lives
don't work.*

I embrace my
inner child with love

Take care of your inner child. It is the child who is frightened. It is the child who is hurting. It is the child who does not know what to do. Be there for your child. Embrace it and love it and do what you can to take care of its needs. Be sure to let your child know that no matter what happens, you will always be there for it. You will never turn away or run away. You will always love this child.

*You
cannot
learn other
people's lessons
for them.
They must
do the work
themselves, and
they will do it when
they are
ready.*

I learn something new everyday

Wouldn't it be wonderful if, instead of having to memo-rize all those battle dates, children were taught how to think, how to love themselves, how to have good relationships, how to be wise parents, how to handle money and how to be healthy. Very few of us have been taught how to handle these different areas of our lives. If we knew, we would do it differently.

*If you still have
a habit that you are
doing, ask yourself how
does it serve you?
What do you get out of it?
If you no longer had it,
what would happen?
Very often people say:*

"My life would be better."

*Why do you believe that
you don't deserve
to have a better
life?*

I let go of the need for this condition in my life

We create habits and patterns because they serve us in some way. Sometimes we are punishing someone or loving someone. It is amazing the number of illnesses created because we want to punish a parent, or love a parent. *"I'm going to have diabetes just like my daddy, because I love my daddy."* It may not always be on a conscious level, but when we start looking within, we will find the pattern. We often create negativity, because we do not know how to handle some area of our lives. We need to ask ourselves: *"What am I feeling sorry about?"* *"Who am I angry at?"* *"What am I trying to avoid?"* *"How will this save me?"* If we are not ready to let something go—really wanting to hold onto it because it serves us—it doesn't matter what we do, it will not work. When we are ready to let it go, it is amazing how the smallest thing can help us release it.

*You
not only
have individual
beliefs, you also
have family and
society's beliefs.
Ideas are
contagious.*

I am good enough

I f there is any belief within you that says: *"You can't have,"* or *"You're not good enough,"* think to yourself: *"I am willing to let that belief go. I do not have to believe that any more."* Please do not struggle. It is not hard work. You are just changing a thought. You were born to enjoy life. Affirm that you are now willing to open to the abundance and prosperity that is available everywhere. You now claim this mentally for yourself right here and right now: *"I deserve to be prosperous. I deserve my good."* That which you have declared is already accomplished in consciousness and now becomes manifest in your experience. And so it is.

*If you have been a very
negative person who criticizes
yourself and everyone
else and sees life
through very
negative eyes,
then it is going to
take time for you to start
turning around and
become loving.
You need to
be patient with
yourself. Don't get angry
with yourself because you
are not doing it
fast enough.*

I declare richness and fullness for my life

I now choose to move away from the limiting beliefs that have been denying me the benefits I so desire. I declare that every negative thought pattern in my consciousness is now being cleared out, erased, and let go. My consciousness is now being filled with cheerful, positive, loving thought patterns that contribute to my health, wealth, and loving relationships. I now release all negative thought patterns that have contributed to fear of loss, fear of the dark, fear of being harmed, fear of poverty, pain, loneliness, self-abuse of any sort, feeling not good enough, burdens or losses of any sort, and any other nonsense that may be lingering in some dark corner of my consciousness. I am now free to allow and accept the good to manifest in my life. I now declare for myself the richness and fullness of life in all its profuse abundance; love lavishly flowing, prosperity abounding, health vital and vibrant, creativity ever new and fresh, and peace all surrounding. All this I deserve and am now willing to accept and have on a permanent basis. I am a co-creator with the One Infinite Allness of Life and therefore the totality of possibilities lie before me and I rejoice that this is so. And so it is!

*Whatever
is happening
out there is only
a mirror of
our own inner
thinking.*

I trust the Intelligence within me

There is One Intelligence. It is everywhere, equally present. This Intelligence is within you and is in everything that you are looking for. When you get lost, or lose something, don't start going into *I am in the wrong place, I won't find my way*. Stop it. Know that the Intelligence within you and the Intelligence in what you are looking for now brings you together. Nothing is ever lost in the Divine Mind. Trust this Intelligence within you.

*One
of the
bonuses
about loving
yourself is that
you get to
feel good.*

My love is limitless

We have so much love in this world, and we have so much love in our hearts, and sometimes we forget. Sometimes we think there isn't enough, or there is just a small amount. So we hoard what we have or we are afraid to let it go. We are afraid to let it out. But those of us who are willing to learn, realize that the more love we allow to flow out from us, the more there is within us and the more we receive. It is endless and timeless. Love is really the most powerful healing force that there is. Without love we could not survive at all. If little tiny babies are not given love and affection, they wither and die. Most of us think we can survive without love, but we cannot. Love for ourselves is the power that heals us. Practice as much as you can.

*At least
three times a day,
stand with your arms
open wide and say:*
"I am willing to let
the love in. It is
safe to let the
love in."

I am worth loving

You don't have to earn love any more than you have to earn the right to breathe. You have a right to breathe because you exist. You have a right to be loved because you exist. That is all you need to know. You are worthy of your own love. Don't allow your parents or society's negative opinions or popular prejudices make you think that you are not good enough. The reality of your being is that you are loveable. Accept this and know this. When you really do, you will find that people treat you as a loveable person.

*Every time you meditate,
every time you do a
visualization for
healing, every time
you say something for
healing the whole planet,
you are connecting with
people who are doing
the same thing.
You are
connecting
with like-minded
people all over the planet.*

I help create a world where it is safe to love each other

It is a dream of mine to help create a world where it is safe for us to love each other—where we can be loved and accepted exactly as we are. It is something we all wanted when we were children—to be loved and accepted exactly as we were. Not when we got taller, or brighter, or prettier, or more like our cousin or sister or the neighbor across the way. But to be loved and accepted exactly as we were. We grow up and want the same—to be loved and accepted exactly as we are right here and right now. But we are not going to get it from other people unless we can give it to ourselves first. When we can love ourselves it becomes easier for us to love other people. When we love ourselves, we don't hurt ourselves and we don't hurt other people. We let go of all prejudices and beliefs about one group or another not being good enough. When we realize how incredibly beautiful we all are, we have the answer to world peace—a world where it is safe for us to love each other.

*If you
believe you did
something wrong,
then you are going
to find a way
to punish
yourself.*

I rise above all limitations

Each experience is a stepping stone in life, including any so-called "mistakes." Love yourself for all your mistakes. They have been very valuable to you. They have taught you many things. It is the way you learn. Be willing to stop punishing yourself for your mistakes. Love yourself for your willingness to learn and grow.

*Have a
good support
group, especially when
you don't want to
do something.
They will help
you grow.*

I have a right to have the life I want

What kind of relationship would you like to have with your mother? Put it into affirmative treatment form and start declaring it for yourself. Then you can tell her. If she is still pushing your buttons, you are not letting her know how you feel. You have a right to have the life you want. You have a right to be an adult. It may not be easy. Decide what it is you need. She may not approve of it, but don't make her wrong. Tell her what you need. Ask her: *"How can we work this out?"* Say to her: *"I want to love you and I want to have a wonderful relationship with you, and I need to be myself."*

*A thought
which says:*

''I'm a bad person,''

*produces a negative feeling.
However, if you do not have
such a thought, you will
not have the feeling.
Change
the thought
and the feeling
must go.*

I am now willing to see only my magnificence

I now choose to eliminate from my mind and life every negative, destructive, fearful idea and thought. I no longer listen to or become part of detrimental thoughts or conversations. Today no one can harm me because I refuse to believe in being hurt. No matter how justified it may seem to be, I refuse to indulge in damaging emotions. I rise above anything that attempts to make me angry or afraid. Destructive thoughts have no power over me. Guilt does not change the past. I think and say only what I want to have created in my life. I am more than adequate for all I need to do. I am one with the power that created me. I am safe. All is well in my world.

*Go for
the joy. Make
that your motto
this year:*

"Go for the joy!
Life is here for
you to enjoy
today!"

This year I do the mental work for change

Many of you start new year resolutions on the first of the year, but because you don't make internal changes, the resolutions fall away very quickly. Until you make the inner changes and are willing to do some mental work, nothing out there is going to change. The only thing you need to change is a thought—only a thought. Even self-hatred is only hating a thought you have about yourself. What can you do for yourself this year in a positive way? What would you like to do for yourself this year that you did not do for yourself last year? What would you like to let go of this year, that you clung to so tightly last year? What would you like to change in your life? Are you willing to do the work that will bring about those changes?

*Observe what is
going on in
your life
and
know that
you are not
your experiences.*

I notice what is going on inside of me

What do you need to do to get to that space where you could be the happiest and most powerful person in your world? If you have done a lot of work on yourself and you understand the principles that what you think and say goes out from you, and the Universe responds and it comes back, then observe yourself. Watch yourself without judgment and without criticism. This seems to be one of the biggest hurdles you have to make. Just look at yourself objectively—all the things about you. Just note what they are without making comments. Just observe. As you allow yourself the space to go inside and begin to notice what is going on—how you feel, how you react, what you believe—you come from a space where you are much more open.

*We can
either destroy the
planet or we can heal it.
It is up to us individually.
Sit down
every day and
send some loving, healing
energy to the planet. What we
do with our minds makes
a difference.*

I am connected to all life

I am spirit, light, energy, vibration, color, and love. I am so much more than I give myself credit for. I am connected with every person on the planet and with all of life. I see myself healthy, whole, and living in a society where it is safe for me to be who I am and to love one another. I hold this vision for myself and for all of us, for this is a time of healing and making whole. I am part of that whole. I am one with all life. And so it is.

*Our
spiritual
growth often
comes to us in
ways that we
don't quite
expect.*

I open new doors to Life

You are standing in the corridor of Life, and behind you so many doors have closed. Things you no longer do, or say, or think. Experiences you no longer have. Ahead of you is a continuous corridor of doors—each one opening to a new experience. So you move away from the past. As you move forward, see yourself opening various doors on wonderful experiences which you would like to have. Trust that your inner guide is leading you and guiding you in ways that are best for you, and that your spiritual growth is continuously expanding. No matter which door opens or which door closes, you are always safe. You are eternal. You will go on forever from experience to experience. See yourself opening doors to joy, peace, healing, prosperity, and love. Doors to understanding, compassion, and forgiveness. Doors to freedom. Doors to self-worth and self-esteem. Doors to self-love. It is all here before you. Which door will you open first? Remember, you are safe, it is only change.

*Fear
comes from
not trusting
the process of life
to be there for you.
The next time you are
frightened, say:*

"I trust
the process
of life to take
care of
me."

All my experiences
are right for me

We have been going through doors since the moment we were born. That was a big door and a big change. We came to this planet to experience life this particular time around. We chose our parents, and we have been through many doors since then. We came equipped with everything within us that we need to live this life fully and richly. We have all the wisdom. We have all the knowledge. We have all the abilities and all the talents. We have all the love and all the emotions that we need. Life is here to support us and take care of us, and we need to know and trust that it is so. Doors are constantly closing and constantly opening, and if we stay centered in ourselves, then we are always safe no matter which doorway we pass through. Even when we pass through the last doorway on this planet, it is not the end. It is the beginning of another new adventure. So let us know that we are always safe. It is alright to experience change. Today is a new day. We will have many wonderful, new experiences. We are loved. We are safe. And so it is.

*Don't
run around
and try to heal
all of your friends.
Do your own mental
work and heal yourself.
This will do more good
for those around you
than anything
else.*

I allow others to be themselves

We cannot force others to change. We can offer them a positive mental atmosphere where they have the possibility to change if they wish. But we cannot do it for or to other people. Each person is here to work out his or her own lessons, and if we fix it for them, then they will just go and do it again, because they have not worked out what they needed to do for themselves. All we can do is love them. Allow them to be who they are. Know that the truth is always within them and that they can change at any moment they want.

*If we
have any
compulsive habit
in any area, instead
of thinking how terrible
we are, let us realize that
there is some need in
our consciousness to
have this condition
or it would not
be there.*

I am safe and secure in my world

Overweight has always meant protection. When you feel insecure, or frightened, you pad yourself with protection. Most of you spend your time being angry at yourselves for being fat and have guilt over food. Weight has nothing to do with the food. There is something going on in your life that is making you feel insecure. You can fight fat for twenty years and still be fat because you have not dealt with the cause. If you are overweight, put the weight issue aside and work on the other issue first—the pattern that says: *"I need protection." "I'm insecure."* Don't get angry when the weight goes on, because our cells respond to our mental patterns. When the need for the protection is gone, or when we start feeling secure, the fat will melt off by itself. Begin to say: *"I used to have a problem with weight."* You will begin to shift the pattern. What you choose to think today will start creating your new figure tomorrow.

*People
who are addicted
are usually running
from themselves, and they
use some sort of addiction
to fill the space
inside.*

I am willing to release my fears

If you are overweight, you can have all the willpower and discipline in the world and go on all sorts of diets. You can be really strong and for months you may not eat one mouthful of food that you *shouldn't* eat. Unfortunately, the moment you drop your willpower and discipline, the weight comes back again. It is because you have not dealt with the real issue. You have only worked on the outer effect. The real issue with weight is usually fear, which creates fat for protection. You can fight fat all your life and never get to the real issue. You could probably die believing you were not good enough because you could not lose the weight. However, your need to feel safe could be fulfilled in a more positive way, then the weight would leave by itself. Say: *"I am willing to release the need for my weight problem. I am willing to release the fear. I am willing to release the need for this protection. I am safe."*

*When we
grow up we
have a tendency
to recreate the emotional
environment of our
early home life.
We tend
to recreate
relationships we
had with our mothers
and fathers or what they
had between
themselves.*

I make my own decisions

Many of you have power-struggle games with your parents. Parents push a lot of buttons. If you *want* to stop playing the game, you are going to *have to* stop playing the game. It is time for you to grow up and decide what you want. You can begin by calling your parents by their first names. Start becoming two adults instead of parent and child.

*It is safe
to look within.
Each time you look
deeper into yourself,
you are going to find
incredibly beautiful
treasures within you.*

I am at the center of peace

The outer world touches me not. I am in charge of my own being. I guard my inner world for it is there that I create. I do whatever I need to do to keep my inner world peaceful. My inner peace is essential for my health and well being. I go within and find that space where all is quiet and serene. I may see it as a peaceful, deep, quiet pool surrounded by green grass and tall, silent trees. I may feel it as white, billowy clouds upon which to lay and be caressed. I may hear it as flowing, delightful music soothing my senses. However I choose to experience my inner space, I find peace. At this center of peace I am. I am the pureness and stillness of the center of my creative process. In peace I create. In peace I live and move and experience life. Because I keep myself centered in inner peace, I have peace in my outer world. Though others may have discord and chaos, it touches me not for I declare peace for myself. Though there may be madness all around me, I am calm and peaceful. The Universe is one of great order and peacefulness, and I reflect this in my every moment of life. The stars and the planets do not need to be worried or fearful in order to maintain their heavenly orbits. Nor does chaotic thinking contribute to my peaceful existence in life. I choose to express peacefulness, for I am peace. And so it is.

*Start listening
to what you say.
If you hear yourself
using negative or
limiting words,
change them.*

I speak and think positively

If you could understand the power of your words, you would be careful about what you say. You would talk constantly in positive affirmations. The Universe always says "yes" to whatever you say, no matter what you choose to believe. If you choose to believe that you are not very much, and life will never be any good, and you will never get anything that you want, the Universe will respond, and that is exactly what you will have. The moment you start to change, the moment you are willing to bring good into your life, the Universe will respond in kind.

Each of us
is doing the
very best we can
at this very moment.
If we knew better, if we
had more understanding
and awareness, we
would do it
differently.

I am totally adequate at all times

Praise yourself and tell yourself how absolutely wonderful you are. Don't make yourself wrong. When you do something new, don't beat yourself because you're not a pro at it the first time. Practice. Learn what does work and doesn't work. Next time you do something new or different, something you are just learning, be there for yourself. Don't tell yourself what was wrong; tell yourself what was right with it. Praise yourself. Build yourself up, so that the next time you do it, you really feel good about it. Each time you will be better and better and better. Soon you will have a new skill of some sort.

*I can
give you
lots of good
advice and lots of
wonderful new ideas,
but you are in
control.
You
can accept
them or not.
You have the power.*

I constantly receive
incredible gifts

L earn to accept prosperity instead of exchanging it. If a friend gives you a gift or takes you to lunch, you don't have to immediately reciprocate. Allow the person to give you the gift. Accept it with joy and pleasure. You may never reciprocate to that person. You may give to someone else. If someone gives you a gift that you can't use or don't want, say: *"I accept with joy and pleasure and gratitude,"* and pass it on to someone else.

*We
are all
teachers
and students.
Ask yourself:*

"What did I come
here to learn and
what did I
come to
teach?"

All of my relationships are enveloped in a circle of love

Envelop your family in a circle of love, whether they are living or not. Include your friends, your loved ones, your spouse, everyone from your work and your past, and all the people you would like to forgive and don't know how. Affirm that you have wonderful, harmonious relationships with everyone, where there is mutual respect and caring on both sides. Know that you can live with dignity and peace and joy. Let this circle of love envelop the entire planet, and let your heart open so you can have a space within you of unconditional love. You are worth loving. You are beautiful. You are powerful. You open yourself to all good. And so it is.

*Relax
and enjoy life.
Know that whatever
you need to know
is revealed
to you
in the perfect
time and space
sequence.*

I am at peace

Today I am a new person. I relax and free my thoughts of every sense of pressure. No person, place, or thing can irritate or annoy me. I am at peace. I am a free person living in a world that is a reflection of my own love and understanding. I am not against anything. I am for everything that will improve the quality of my life. I use my words and my thoughts as tools to shape my future. I express gratitude and thanksgiving often and look for things to be thankful for. I am relaxed. I live a peaceful life.

Take a
nice, deep breath
and release the
resistance.

I am willing to release the need for this condition

No matter how long your negative beliefs have been in your subconscious, affirm now that you are free of them. Affirm that you are willing to release the causes, the patterns in your consciousness that are creating any negative conditions in your life right now. Affirm that you are now willing to release the need for these conditions. Know that they disappear, fade away, and dissolve back into the nothingness from whence they came. The old garbage no longer has a hold on you. You are free! And so it is.

*How often do
you go into yesterday's
mental garbage to create
tomorrow's experiences?
You need to periodically do
some mental housecleaning
and toss out the old rubbish,
or the things that no longer
suit you or no longer
fit you.
You want to polish
those ideas which are
positive and good and
that nourish you and use
them more often.*

I release the past with ease and I trust the process of life

Close the door on old, painful memories. Close the door on old hurts, old self righteous unforgiveness. You might take an incident in the past where there was pain and hurt— something that is hard for you to forgive or look at. Ask yourself: *"How long do I want to hold onto this? How long do I want to suffer because of something that happened in the past?"* Now see a stream in front of you and take this old experience, this hurt, this pain, this unforgiveness, and put the whole incident in the stream and see it begin to dissolve and drift downstream until it totally dissipates and disappears. You do have the ability to let go. You are free. And so it is.

*We resist
the most that which
we most need to learn.
If you keep saying:*

"I can't," *or* "I won't,"

*you are probably
referring to a lesson
that is important
to you.*

I am wonderful and I feel great

Reprograming your negative beliefs is very powerful. A good way to do it is by making a tape with your own voice on it. Your own voice means a lot to you. Make a tape of your affirmations and play it. It will have a great deal of value for you. If you want a tape that is even more powerful, have your mother make a tape for you. Can you imagine going to sleep with your mother telling you how wonderful you are, how much she loves you, how proud she is of you, and how she knows you can be anything in this world?

*Resentment,
criticism, guilt
and fear come from
blaming others and not
taking responsibility
for our own
experiences.*

I am motivated by love

Release from within you all bitterness and resentment. Affirm that you are totally willing to freely forgive everyone. If you think of anyone who may have harmed you in any way at any point in your lifetime, you now bless that person with love and release him. And dismiss the thought. Nobody can take anything from you that is rightfully yours. That which belongs to you will always return to you in Divine right order. If something does not come back to you, then it isn't meant to. Accept this with peace. Dissolving resentment is highly important. Trust yourself. You are safe. You are motivated by love.

*It is very
comfortable
to play victim,
because it is always
somebody else's fault.
You have to stand on your
own two feet and take
some responsibility.*

I have the power to make changes

There is a difference between responsibility and blame. When we talk about responsibility, we are really talking about *having power*. When we talk about blame, we are talking about *making wrong*. Responsibility is a gift because it gives you the power to make changes. Unfortunately, some people choose to interpret it as guilt. These people usually accept everything as a guilt trip in one way or another, because it is another way to make themselves wrong. Being a victim is wonderful on one level because then everyone else is responsible and we don't get a chance to make changes. When people insist on feeling guilty, there is not much we can do about it. They either accept the information or they don't. Just leave them alone. We are not responsible for their feeling guilty.

*We never
get even.
Revenge
does not work,
because what you
give out comes
back to you.
The buck
has to stop
somewhere.*

I release all old hurts and forgive myself

When you hold onto the past with bitterness and anger and don't allow yourself to experience the present moment, you are wasting today. If you hold onto bitterness and grudges for a long time, it has to do with forgiving yourself, not the other person. If you hold onto old hurts, you punish yourself in the here and now. Often, you sit in a prison of self-righteous resentment. Do you want to be right, or do you want to be happy? Forgive yourself and stop punishing yourself.

*Choose
to believe
that it is easy
to change a
thought or
a pattern.*

I always have choice

Most of us have foolish ideas about who we are and many rigid rules about how life *should* be lived. Let's remove the word *"should"* from our vocabulary forever. *Should* is a word that makes a prisoner of us. Every time we use *should* we are making ourselves wrong, or we are making someone else wrong. We are in effect saying, *"not good enough."* What can be dropped now from your *should* list? Replace the word *"should"* with the word *"could." Could* lets you know that you have choice, and choice is freedom. We need to be aware that everything we do in life is done by choice. There is really nothing that we have to do. We always have choice.

*We operate
with ten percent
of our brains.
What is the other
ninety percent for?
Think about that.
How much
more can we
know?*

I give over my problems and sleep peacefully

Sleep is a time to restore ourselves and wrap up the day. Our bodies repair themselves and become renewed and refreshed. Our minds move into the dream state where problems of the day are solved. We prepare ourselves for the new day ahead. As we enter the sleep state we want to take positive thoughts with us—thoughts that will create a wonderful new day and a wonderful new future. So if there is any anger or blame in you, let it go. If there is any resentment or fear, let it go. If there is any jealousy or rage, let it go. If there is any guilt or need for punishment lingering in the corners of your mind, let it go. Feel only peace in your mind and body as you drift off to sleep.

We create habits
and problems to
fulfill a need within us.
When we can find
a positive way
to fulfill the
need, we
can release
the problem.

There is a solution
to every problem

For every problem I create there is a solution. I am not limited by my human-mind thinking for I am connected with the entire Universal Wisdom and Knowledge. I come from the loving space of the heart and know that love opens all doors. There is an ever-ready Power that helps me meet and overcome every challenge and crisis in my life. I know that every problem has been healed somewhere in the world. Therefore, I know that this can happen for me. I wrap myself in a cocoon of love and I am safe. All is well in my world.

*Every time you hear
something is incurable,
know in your mind
that it isn't true.
Know there is
a Power
greater.*

Infinite Spirit is eternal

The sun is always shining. Even though clouds may come along and obscure the sun for awhile, the sun is always shining. The sun never stops shining. And even though the earth turns, and the sun appears to go down, it really never stops shining. The same is true of Infinite Power and Infinite Spirit. It is eternal. It is always here, always giving light to us. We may obscure its presence by the clouds of negative thinking, but that Spirit, that Power, that healing energy is always with us.

*In order
to reprogram
the subconscious mind,
you need to relax the body.
Release the tension.
Let the emotions go.
Get to a state of
openness and
receptivity.
You are
always in charge.
You are always safe.*

My life is a joy

Your subconscious mind does not know true from false or right from wrong. You never want to say something like: *"Oh, stupid old me,"* because the subconscious mind picks up on it, and after you say it awhile, you begin to feel that way. You begin to believe what you are saying. Don't joke about yourself, deprecate yourself, or make derogatory remarks about life, because that is not going to create good experiences for you.

*When good comes
into our lives
and we deny
it by saying:*

"I don't believe it,"

*we literally push
our good
away.*

I dwell on positive thoughts

I magine that thoughts are like drops of water. When you think the same thoughts over and over again, you are creating this incredible body of water. First you have a little puddle, then you may get a pond, and as you continue to think the same thoughts over and over and over again, you have a lake, and finally an ocean. If your thoughts are negative, you can drown in a sea of your own negativity. If your thoughts are positive, you can float on the ocean of life.

*The work
you are doing
on yourself is not
a goal, it is a process—
a lifetime process.
Enjoy the
process.*

I am here at the right time

We are all on an endless journey through eternity and the time we spend on this plane of action is but a brief instant. We choose to come to this planet to learn lessons and to work on our spiritual growth, and to expand our capacity to love. There is no right time and no wrong time to come and go. We always come in the middle of the movie and we leave in the middle of the movie. We leave when our particular task is finished. We come to learn to love ourselves more and to share that love with all those around us. We come to open our hearts on a much deeper level. Our capacity to love is the only thing we take with us when we leave. If you left today, how much would you take?

*If you
don't trust
other people,
it is because you
are not there for yourself.
You don't support yourself.
You don't back yourself up.
When you really begin to
be there for you, then you
will trust yourself, and when
you trust yourself,
you will trust
other people.*

I am connected
with the Higher Power

Now is the time for you to learn about your own power, and what you are capable of doing. What can you let go of? What can you nourish within you? What can you newly create? The wisdom and intelligence of the Universe is yours to use. Life is here to support you. If you get scared, think of your breath, and be aware of each breath as it goes in and out of your body. Your breath is the most precious substance in your life, and it is so freely given to you. You have enough to last for as long as you shall live. If this most precious substance is so freely given, so that you can accept it without even thinking, can you not trust life to supply you with the other things you need?

*You are
in the process
of becoming your own
best friend—the person
you are most joyous
to be with.*

I love and accept
myself right now

Many of you will not love yourselves until you lose weight, get a new job, a lover, this or that. So you always put loving yourself off. What happens when you get the new job, or the lover, or you lose weight, and you still don't love yourself? You just make another list, and you have another delay period. The only time you can begin to love who you are is right here and right now. Unconditional love is love with no expectations. It is accepting what is.

*We are on the
cutting edge of a
new consciousness
awakening for the
whole planet.
How far
are you willing
to expand the horizons
of your thinking?*

I am one with everyone on the planet

I do not believe in two powers, of good and evil. I think there is One Infinite Spirit and there are human beings who have the opportunity to use the intelligence and wisdom and tools they have been given in every way. When you talk about *them*, you are always talking about *us*, because we are the people, we are the government, we are the churches, and we are the planet. The place to begin making changes is right where we are. I think it is all too easy to say: *"It's the devil." "It's them."* It really is always *us*!

*When we
grow up, we
get so worried about
what the neighbors think.
We say to ourselves:*

"Will they approve of me?"

*Everybody and everything is
unique and different and
meant to be that way.
If we are
like other people,
then we are not expressing
our own specialness.*

I am my own unique self

You are not your father. You are not your mother. You are not any of your relatives. You are not your teachers at school, nor are you the limitations of your early religious training. You are *yourself*. You are special and unique, having your own set of talents and abilities. No one can do things exactly the way you can do them. There is no competition and no comparison. You are worthy of your own love and your own self-acceptance. You are a magnificent being. You are free. Acknowledge this as the new truth for yourself. And so it is.

*If you
are going to
listen to people,
listen to the winners.
Listen to the people who
know what they are
doing and who
prove what
they are
doing.*

I am a natural winner

As we learn to love ourselves we become powerful. Our love for ourselves moves us from being victims to being winners. Our love for ourselves attracts to us wonderful experiences. People who feel good about themselves are naturally attractive because they have an aura about them that is just wonderful. They are always winning at Life. We can be willing to learn to love ourselves. We can be winners, too.

*Meditation
is really just
quieting yourself
enough so you can
get in touch
with your
own inner
wisdom.*

I follow my inner wisdom

Come from that wonderful, caring spot of your heart. Stay centered and love who you are and know that you really are a Divine, Magnificent Expression of Life. No matter what is going on *out there*, you are centered. You have a right to your feelings. You have a right to your opinions. You just are. You work on loving yourself. You work on opening your heart. You work on doing what is right for you and getting in touch with your inner voice. Your inner wisdom knows the answers for you. Sometimes it is scary to do that, because the answer you get inside may be quite different than what your friends want you to do. Yet you know inwardly what is right for you. And if you follow this inner wisdom, you are at peace with your own being. Support yourself in making the right choices for yourself. When you are in doubt, ask yourself: *"Am I coming from the loving space of the heart? Is this a decision that is loving for me? Is this right for me now?"* The decision you make at some later point, a day, a week, or a month later, may no longer be the right choice, and then you can change it. Ask in every moment: *"Is this right for me?"* And say: *"I love myself and I am making the right choices."*

*Procrastination
is another form
of resistance.*

I am working at a career that I really enjoy

What do you think about your work? Do you think of it as drudgery that you *have to* do, or do you see it as something you really love to do and enjoy? Begin to affirm that what you do is very fulfilling to you. You get pleasure from your work. You connect with the creativity of the Universe and allow it to flow through you in fulfilling ways. Affirm this every time negative thoughts come up about your work.

*Everything
in our lives is a
mirror of us.
When something
is happening* out there
*that is not comfortable,
we have to look
inside and say:*

"How am I creating it?
What is it within me that
believes I deserve
this experience?"

I have the perfect space

I see myself filled with gratitude and thanksgiving as I walk through this facility. I see the perfect space and equipment for mailing and shipping, the business offices laid out perfectly, an area just the right size for meetings. All the equipment needed is in its place and the staff is a group of harmonious, dedicated people. The offices are beautiful, orderly and peaceful. I rejoice in the work being done to aid in soul growth, and the healing and harmonizing of our world. I see, open receptive souls drawn to the activities sponsored by this facility. I am thankful for the ever-flowing abundant supply to this facility to support its mission. And so it is.

*If you
choose to believe:*

"Everyone is always helpful,"

*you will find that
wherever you go
in life, people are there
to help you.*

Each person is part
of the harmonious whole

We are each a divine idea expressing through the One Mind in harmonious ways. We have come together because there is something we need to learn from each other. We have a purpose in being together. There is no need to fight this purpose or to blame one another for what is happening. It is safe for us to work on loving ourselves so that we may benefit and grow from this experience. We choose to work together to bring harmony into the business at hand and into every area of our own lives. Everything we do is based on the one truth—the truth of our beings and the truth of Life. Divine right action is guiding us every moment of the day. We say the right word at the right time and follow the right course of action at all times. Each person is part of the harmonious whole. There is a Divine blending of energies as people work joyfully together, supporting and encouraging each other in ways that are fulfilling and productive. We are successful in every area of our work and our lives. We are healthy, happy, loving, joyful, respectful, supportive, productive, and at peace with ourselves and with each other. This treatment is lovingly released into the One Mind which does the work and makes it manifest in our lives. So be it, and so it is. It is done!

In the Aquarian Age
we are learning to
go within to
find our savior.
We are the power
we are looking for.
Each one of us
is totally linked
with the Universe
and with Life.

This world is our heaven on earth

I see a community of spiritually-minded souls who come together to share, grow and radiate their energies into the world—each one free to pursue his or her activity and drawn together to better fulfill each individual's purpose. I see us guided to form the new heaven on earth with others who have the same desire to prove to themselves and others that it can be now. We live together harmoniously, lovingly, peacefully, expressing God in our lives and our living. We establish a world where the nurturing of soul growth is the most important activity, where this is the work of the individual. There is ample time and opportunity for creative expression in whatever area we choose. There will be no labor and no concern for earning money. All that we need we will be able to express through the powers within. Education will be a process of remembering that which we already know and bring to conscious awareness. There is no disease, no poverty, no crime, and no deceit. The world of the future begins now, right here, with all of us. And so it is.

Personal Notes

Personal Notes

Personal Notes

Personal Notes

Personal Notes

Personal Notes

Personal Notes

Personal Notes

Personal Notes

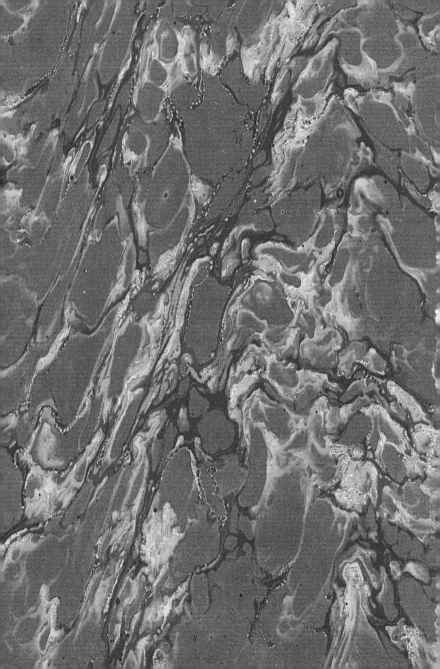